JUSTINE

Borgo Press Dramas by FRANK J. MORLOCK

JUSTINE

A PLAY IN THREE ACTS

FRANK J. MORLOCK

Adapted from the Novel by the Marquis de Sade

THE BORGO PRESS

MMXII

JUSTINE

FIRST BORGO PRESS EDITION

Published by Wildside Press LLC

www.wildsidebooks.com

DEDICATION

To the memory of my mother,

Eva Pierson Morlock,

whose virtue was as obstinate as Justine's, but fortunately never exposed to Justine's misfortunes

CONTENTS

JUSTINE

CAST OF CHARACTERS

The Marquis de Sade
Justine, a pious virgin
Juliette, her sister
Landlady
Hairpin
First Man
Second Man
Third Man
Fourth Man
Florent, a wealthy noble
Young Man
Servant
Brother Severino
Second Monk
Third Monk
Fourth Monk
Doctor Rodin
Rosalie
Brother Martin
Judge
Hangman
M. de Corville

Madame Dubois

First Actor: De Sade, Hairpin, Brother Severino, Doctor Rodin

Second Actor: First Man, Second Monk, Brother Martin

Third Actor: Second Man, Third Monk, Hangman

Fourth Actor: Third Man, Servant, Third Monk, Hangman

Fifth Actor: Fourth Man, Servant, Fourth Monk, M. de Corville

Sixth Actor: Florent, Judge

Seventh Actor: Young Man

First Actress: Justine

Second Actress: Juliette, Rosalie, Young Man

Third Actress: Landlady, Madame Dubois, Countess

AUTHOR'S NOTE

It is possible, and even desirable, for doubling the characters in this play. When doubling occurs, very little effort should be made to conceal the identity of the actor. Presumably, this will produce a somewhat dream-like effect. Nine or ten players are all that is necessary. The part of the young man may be played by a woman. If so, only nine actors are needed.

As to costumes, no great effort for realism should be made, however, powdered wigs are in order for de Sade, Hairpin, Florent, Rodin, and Corville. Juliette should have as elegant a wig and gown as possible.

PROLOGUE
SCENE 1

The scenery should be as garish and lurid as possible, but no effort at realism is needed. Rather, the scenery should have the effect of a nightmare; i.e., details should be out of proportion, or occasionally, but not always, fantastic.

Enter the Marquis, before the curtain goes up.

De Sade

Allow me to introduce myself, ladies and gentlemen. You see before you a much maligned and traduced old man. I am at your service, the Marquis de Sade. I belong to an illustrious house, but alas, we have fallen on sad days, and my enemies have triumphed over me, and spread, quite successfully, the rumor that I am insane.

One young man has recently gone so far as to slander my name by ascribing a tragedy to me called *Marat* which he then styles as 'produced by the Marquis de Sade and the inmates of Charenton.' It is most unkind to make reference to my unfortunate sojourn in that institution. Most ungentlemanly. I was put there for political, not hygienic reasons. In fact, the whole thing was engineered to discredit my work. A trick not altogether forgotten in modern times.

At any rate, this play *Marat*, which has attracted so much attention, has raised suspicions that not only is the author mad, but so are those who would act in his play. (bowing) That is most untrue. In order to rebut this libel, a young friend of mine has undertaken to dramatize a trifle of mine known as 'Justine.' The young scamp has toned down some of the scenes and made some necessary adjustments to fit modern taste. But, I pronounce this play fully in the spirit of the original. Far from finding my characters insane, you will see that they behave in accordance with the highest standards of rationality set by the age and do nothing but upon philosophic reflection of the most refined kind.

And, as for the actors, they too, are quite sane. So I shall demonstrate by acting the part of a noted surgeon in this morality.

Let the play begin. (he bows again)

The Curtain Rises

ACT I
SCENE 2

A poor garret in Paris in the years preceding the Revolution. A staircase leading up to it. Juliette sits at a shabby mirror primping. Justine, her sister, enters from the stairs. Both are pretty aristocrats who have fallen on hard times.

Juliette

Well, did you find any work, Justine?

Justine

Leave me alone, Juliette.

Juliette

There just isn't much a girl of sixteen can do—is there?

Justine

We'll find something. Tomorrow, for sure.

Juliette

You've been saying that for a month.

Justine

We mustn't give up hope. We aren't starving yet.

Juliette

We will be if you don't start to use your head.

Justine

What do you mean?

Juliette

It's rather simple, isn't it? We're both well-born, educated, and pretty. We're both virgins. Now, it's true enough we are poor; but we weren't always so. Until father was ruined we received an aristocratic education. As such, we are an asset to any man. There are dozens of men in the city of Paris who would be delighted to—

Justine

I suppose we should just walk up to them and say, 'Marry me,' and they will be delighted and say, 'I should be delighted.' You are so impractical, Juliette! Why don't you be realistic? We'll have to earn our bread. We can't be proud.

Juliette

My dear girl, I am very realistic. We can hardly expect them to marry us.

Justine

Well, then—oh, you can't mean that! My sister!

Juliette

Now, who's being proud? After all, isn't it better to be immoral than to be a scullion?

Justine

Juliette! It is far preferable to be a scrubwoman than to be a lady of leisure who is a prostitute.— From any moral point of view.

Juliette

But from an aesthetic one? Oh, darling Justine, when I see my own sister being so silly!

Justine

Father wouldn't have approved this.

Juliette

So much the better that he is dead.

Justine

You don't mean that.

Juliette

I certainly do! Father got us into this mess by his foolish investments. If he were here he would prevent us from taking the necessary measures to get ourselves out of it. Now, we are governed only by our inclinations, and mine, dear sister, are very carefree. Think of the happy opportunity our poverty gives us to indulge in vices that we should never dare to experience were we rich. Why, if father had lived and kept his fortune, we should have been bullied into respectability. But now, darling, we can let ourselves go.

Justine

I don't want to hear any more of this.

Juliette

Please yourself. I'm going for a walk. (she flounces out)

Justine

This is just talk, I know, Julie, but it upsets me so—

please— She's gone. (Justine kneels before a crucifix) Dear God, I pray to you to aid us in our affliction, and bring us comfort in our sorrow. Lead us not into temptation. I swear and vow that I shall never take the path my sister has seen fit to jest about. Forgive her, the words she spoke in despair. Dear God, I pray to you for our salvation. I await your sign.

(The room is illuminated momentarily as with a holy light, then the landlady enters.)

Landlady

You got the rent?

Justine

You know I haven't. Oh, if you'd just be patient.

Landlady

Why should I be patient?

Justine

Something will turn up soon. I've been praying. God will answer my prayers.

Landlady

Well, maybe he will at that. I don't want yez to think I ain't got no feelings. I told your story to a man who is a regular phil-anthropist. He said he'd like to see you.

Justine

Oh, this must be God's answer.

Landlady

He's waiting on the stairs. Shall I tell him to come in?

Justine

Oh, do.

Landlady

He's easy to get around. Butter him up now. You can come in now, Mr. Hairpin.

(The Landlady exits and Hairpin enters. Hairpin is the same actor that plays the Marquis.)

Justine (falling at his feet)

Alas, I am a poor orphan. I am only sixteen and I am nearly starving. I beg you to have pity on me.

Hairpin

That's a shame. That's a shame. I'm an old man but I have a soft heart. A soft heart.

Justine

Oh, sir, I can see it.

Hairpin

Are you a good girl?

Justine

Oh, sir—would I be in such a state if I were not?

Hairpin

That answer pleases me. I have a weakness for virgins. Yes, I confess it. A weakness for virgins. It comes from being old and having a soft heart.

Justine

Oh, I know you will do something for me.

Hairpin

I have just one more question I should like to ask you. Are you resolved to remain a good girl?

Justine

Oh, yes, sir.

Hairpin

That answer is not pleasing to me. Perhaps, you misunderstand me and think me to be some sort of fool who meant to give you aid in mere charity.

Justine

Yes, sir. I thought you were so good.

Hairpin

Just because I am old and have a soft heart, do you think I have a soft head?

Justine (sobbing)

Oh, sir.

Hairpin

There, there. I do not wish to be unkind. Undoubtedly, you took me for a religious fool and gave the answer you thought would please me. I do not despise you for such hypocrisy. I simply wish to straighten things out. Now, I ask you again. Are you resolved to remain a good girl?

Justine

Yes, sir. More than ever.

Hairpin

You don't think I am trying to test you, do you? You believe me, that I am serious.

Justine

Yes.

Hairpin

Then, by what right do you expect the rich to help you if you will not serve them?

Justine

I shall be happy to serve you in any proper way.

Hairpin

I am an old man, and I have a soft heart. But, I tell you truly, there is but one proper way you can serve me and that is with your body.

Justine

Dear God, is there no charity left among men?

Hairpin

I give that I may receive. Charity is nothing but the enjoyment of pride, and I hate pride.

Justine

Sir, with principles like these the poor must perish.

Hairpin

Let them. There are more people around than necessary as it is.

Justine

Do you believe children could respect their parents if they were treated like this?

Hairpin

What do children mean to a parent when they are troublesome?

Justine

They'd be better off smothered in the cradle.

Hairpin

Of course. Such has been the salutary custom in many countries. Soon we shall revive it here. Why let bastards and cripples burden the tax rolls? I look forward to the day when a perfectly rational economy will forbid charity and decree starvation for those who were so ignorant as to be born poor.

Justine (sobbing)

Oh, sir, it's hard to be an orphan.

Hairpin

Why complain when it lies within your power to improve your situation?

Justine

At what price!

Hairpin

I shall not be stingy.

Justine

Beast! May heaven punish you as you deserve.

Hairpin (leaving)

I hate beggars.

(Enter Landlady.)

Landlady

You stupid little bitch. Think what you are doing.

Hairpin

I am an old man with a soft heart. She hasn't treated me right. She made me so unhappy. (Hairpin wobbles toward the stairs)

Landlady

You fool! Do something!

Justine

What do you expect me to do?

Landlady

Go to him. Make it up with him. Whatever you do, behave like a lady.

Justine

Never.

(Hairpin wobbles downstairs and meets Juliette returning.)

Juliette

Have you seen my sister?

Hairpin

If that young slut is your sister, the answer is 'yes.'

Juliette

What is wrong?

Hairpin

I am an old man, with a soft—how old are you?

Juliette

Just sixteen, sir.

Hairpin

And, you have been a good girl?

Juliette

Oh, yes sir. (winking at him)

Hairpin

I might do something for such a girl, if—

Juliette

If she were not determined to remain a good girl—?

Hairpin

Charming child. You read my mind. But, I should want proof that you have been a good girl till now.

Juliette

Sir, you can easily prove it yourself. I am prepared to submit to the most rigorous test.

Hairpin

Sweet angel. Will you be kind?

Juliette

No. I shall be very cruel. But, I am prepared to give every satisfaction.

Hairpin (exiting with Juliette)

Ah, I am so old—and my heart is so soft.

Landlady (to Justine)

As for you—since you're so stubborn, you can go to jail for not paying the rent.

Blackout

ACT I

SCENE 3

A road and some woods nearby. Justine, an old lady, and several men enter. All are shabbily dressed. Madame Dubois is played by the same actress who plays the Landlady.

Madame Dubois

There, my darling, we can rest here. We're free as birds.

Justine

Oh, but think how we escaped from jail.

Madame Dubois

It can't be helped. Setting fire to the jail was the only way out.

Justine

But, all those prisoners who were burned to death!

Madame Dubois

What do we care as long as we made our escape? That's their tough luck.

Justine

Oh, Madame Dubois, I owe you my freedom, but truly, I'd rather have died myself than do it.

Madame Dubois

Well, if you're squeamish, console yourself with the thought that you couldn't prevent it. It wouldn't have done you any good to stay there and burn.

Justine

I suppose.

Madame Dubois

Anyway, now that you're free, what will you do?

Justine

Look for a job, I guess.

Madame Dubois

I could find you a cozy little place in a house I own in Marseilles.

Justine

I can only do maid work; I don't know how to cook.

Madame Dubois

Not as a cook, dear. Oh, this child, she's so innocent. Just like myself at her age. As a prostitute.

Justine

I'm sorry, Madame Dubois. I'm grateful to you, but I shall never sacrifice my religion or my chastity. I shall be rewarded for my virtue in a better world. Such thoughts console me in distress.

Madame Dubois

Stuff and nonsense. Don't you see this virtue of yours is an invention of the rich to keep the poor in their place?

Justine

That's not true.

Madame Dubois

Believe what you like. I just hope you don't fall victim to that irony of fate which rewards crime at the price of virtue.

First Man

Hey, Justine.

Justine

Yes.

First Man

Madame Dubois tells us as how you ain't never had a man before.

Justine (blushing)

That's true.

Second Man

Hey, what you know about that?

Third Man

See, I told you, didn't I?

Fourth Man

Take a look at her. Kind of frightened like.

First Man

How old are you, Justine?

Justine

I'm nearly seventeen.

Second Man

It ain't right for a girl to go that long without a man.

Third Man

It's unnatural.

Fourth Man

It's against God's will.

Justine

Don't blaspheme.

First Man

We figure, Justine, it's our duty to pleasure you, take care of you. Any one of us.

Fourth Man

All of us.

Third Man

Yeah. Like you was our sister.

First Man

You just go ahead and choose, or if you just can't make up your mind between us 'cos we're all so good looking, we'll flip a coin. Or take turns.

Second Man

You just go ahead and pick out the lucky guy.

Fourth Man

I hope you like me, Justine. I ain't never had a girl said she was a virgin.

Third Man

I had one said she was. What a liar!

Justine

I don't want any of you.

Fourth Man

That's kind of unfriendly. You choose or we'll choose for you.

Justine

Madame Dubois, help me. Save me.

Madame Dubois

You sure are dumb. I wouldn't refuse any of them. Four such strapping boys.

Justine

I'll do anything—but save me.

Madame Dubois

Okay. I'm boss here. You fellows leave her alone.

First Man

Ah—

Madame Dubois (drawing a dagger)

Shut up, you moron, or I'll cut your heart out.

First Man

But, I just wanted to fool around with her.

Madame Dubois

That's well enough. But what I say goes. Don't brook my authority. We'll use her for our interests, not our pleasure. We can use her fresh little maidenhead to catch suckers.

First Man

All right for that. But, she must satisfy us—in a different way.

Justine

What do you mean?

Madame Dubois

The boys have some strange ideas of fun.

(The bandits lay hold on her. They pull off her clothes, until she is nearly naked. Then, they twist her hands behind her back.)

First Man

You look swell, Justine, really. You don't know how pretty you look. Come on, wench, implore your God! Beg him to come and save you. Let's see if he really can do it.

(One of the men throws a noose over the limb of a tree.)

First Man

Come on, pray girl, you haven't much time. The curtain is going up in a minute.

Fourth Man (putting the noose around her neck)

We're not playing, Justine.

Justine

Dear God, forgive them for—

First Man (tightening the noose)

This torture is sweeter than you think. You will feel death through exquisite sensations of pleasure. Tightening of the noose will set all your nerves on fire.

(Justine emits a strangled scream.)

First Man

Yell louder. (jerking the noose)

Justine

Aieee!

First Man

Louder.

(Justine screams faintly.)

First Man

Now, Justine, tell us the truth. Wasn't that fun? Not

that it matters though to us. It's our pleasure we're interested in. It was so good that I'm going to try a variation on it.

Justine

Why don't you just kill me? Kill me, I beg of you.

Madame Dubois

And, why should we? By what right do you ask us to ease your lot?

First Man

Why should we? We ask nothing from you. I make use of a woman from necessity, as I make use of a vase— in a different necessity. We owe you nothing.

Justine

Oh sir, to what height do you carry your wickedness?

First Man

To the highest point, Justine, to the highest point. Crime kindles my lust. Without it, I am impotent.

Justine

From which I deduce you are an ill man.

First Man

From which I deduce that to be healthy, I must commit crime. It is not your body that I love, but the idea of the wrong I do you when I love it, that throws me into ecstasy. The more heinous the crime, the more delightful the act.

Madame Dubois

Truly, Justine, don't you think the proposition these boys offered you was preferable to this?

Justine

No.

Madame Dubois

Aha. So, you're a masochist. I thought as much.

First Man

Put that barrel under her feet. Now, you stand on it, Justine.

(The barrel is rolling slightly; one of the bandits tightens and shortens the noose. Justine must keep walking around to prevent the barrel from rolling from under her.)

First Man

Pretty soon, I'm going to push the barrel from under you. Be careful, Justine, it may get away from you. (to the others) Now, perhaps, we can have some sensible conversation with her. (to Justine) Now, Justine, once again I offer you a choice. Give yourself to me, dear, and I'll save you from this riff raff—and from death.

Justine

I, sir! I, become the mistress of a—

First Man

Don't be afraid, say it. 'Thief.' 'Murderer.' Is it not? Well, it's the best offer you're likely to get. Isn't it better to give yourself up to one man, who will be your protector, than to prostitute yourself with all?

Justine

But, why must I do either?

First Man

Oh, I'm going to pull it out from under you, really I am. I'll try to be patient because right is with the strong and you are weak.

Madame Dubois

How can you be so simple as to believe virtue depends upon a little more or a little less of skin? Silly child!

Justine

I will remain a virgin or die.

Madame Dubois

Misguided girl. Woman was designed for man's pleasure and her own. Nature intends that all living creatures do what they were designed for. It is criminal of you to resist your function.

First Man

Never mind all that religious bunk. Look Justine, to hell with your virginity. You can keep it. A woman has more than one favor to bestow on a man. We shall be content with that. Need I say more?

Justine

Say no more, indeed.

Second Man

The girl's a pervert.

Third Man

Hang her for a witch.

Justine

Don't you realize that God punishes man for such a crime as the worst of all. Sex was only meant to beget children.

Madame Dubois

What nonsense. Who told you that? The proof that what you say is not true lies in our ability to do something else with it.

First Man

How do you know that the purpose of sex was not pleasure, rather than propagation, since the first is, after all, a more frequent result than the latter?

Justine

God attached pleasure to the act so that—

Madame Dubois

So that we should be tempted to propagate, no doubt. But, we are prompted to do other things as well, my dear. For propagation is, after all, not very tempting.

Second Man

If that was God's purpose, he made a mess of it.

Third Man

As if nothing but physical pleasure could induce people to want children.

First Man

As if people who don't want children could be induced to it by a physical pleasure that may be attained in so many others ways.

Third Man

Let's send her flying.

Justine

Oh, don't you feel heaven's condemnation written in your own words?

Madame Dubois

The only feelings that stop people are moral feelings. And, it is a peculiarity of moral feelings that they are always false. It is only propaganda that prevents you from doing great deeds.

Justine

How can you say that? Mankind will unite against you. Why, what would be the result if your gang were to operate on such principles? Why they would cut your throat.

Madame Dubois

What you say, sweet Justine, is only apparently true. It is our self interest that stays our hand. But, in your case, for example, what interest has society in you, if you have nothing to offer? I find no fault in the arrangement. But, I firmly believe that the underdog should never submit to it. There is no reward for the weak unless they turn to crime.

Justine

And, what of the bliss of paradise? You can't take that away from us.

First Man

Bunk. You can take it if it gives you any consolation. The poor must suffer; it's one of nature's laws. But it's not a law of nature that I must be poor.

Madame Dubois

The poor are necessary so that wealth may be created by exploiting them.

Justine

Horrid principle.

Madame Dubois

My dear Justine, stealing is one of the chief means of reestablishing an equality of wealth.

Third Man

In some countries, theft is even honored as a noble deed.

Fourth Man

Unfortunately, in the present lamentable state of society, there is an attempt to prevent the operation of natural law by keeping all the wealth in the hands of the rich without making any concessions to natural skill and cunning.

First Man

Which is why we are outlaws.

Second Man

Through no fault of nature, but merely on account of man-made law.

Justine

But, all this may be redressed. Soon, there will be a revolution—. There is talk of it. And then, there will be equality and food for all.

Madame Dubois

What drivel! A revolution is fine. We'll profit by it, no doubt. But you cannot change nature. Nature has decreed that there shall be poverty. The reason nature has decreed this is that she knows poverty will drive us to crime. And this is nature's scheme.

Justine

Blasphemy!

Madame Dubois

The girl is a theologian.

Third Man

I knew she was a witch.

Fourth Man

Let's hang her.

First Man

Here, Justine. Here is a knife. I'm going to pull the barrel out from under you. If you cut the rope in time, you shall live. But, you must not cut it before I remove the barrel—if you do, I'll hang you in earnest. Now, while Madame Dubois delivers you a sermon, I'll choose the right moment to set you dangling.

Justine

Dear God, Who art in Heaven, comfort me.

Madame Dubois

Ah, you will talk theology. God is a creation of the mind—the mind which cannot understand natural law, because the mind has not yet reached the stage of detecting natural patterns or because it lacks the courage to acknowledge what it sees.

Justine (to herself)

God is good. He has created the lilies of the field, and—

Madame Dubois

If God is good, and everything is good, what else can He do? Or, if things are not good, then He, of necessity, must be bad,—which is a view I incline to.

First Man (kicking the barrel from beneath her)

Now, Justine! (Justine succeeds, after a struggle, in cutting the rope) Well, how did it feel? You did it, after all. Make another noose. (the two other men make a noose) Did it hurt, Justine? Did it?

Justine (dazed)

I don't know, I—

First Man

I'll bet it didn't. I want to find out for myself. I know a noose awaits me if I am ever captured, so I am going to find out what it's like in advance. (he strips off his shirt and down to his bare chest) You shall do to me what I did to you. (he stands on the barrel) I'm going to masturbate. You let me hang till you see my pleasure coming, or symptoms of pain. Then, cut me down. (he kicks the barrel away)

Justine

You're crazy.

First Man (in a strangled voice)

Oh, Justine. No one has any idea of the feeling. It's inexpressibly delicious— Now cut me down.

(Justine moves in to cut the rope, but Madame Dubois

knocks her down.)

Madame Dubois (pulling a pistol)

No one touch him.

First Man (strangled)

Why?

Madame Dubois

You've been questioning my authority of late. I was looking for an opportunity of ridding myself of you. Well, what could be more convenient than this?

(His legs have been kicking wildly, but now he is dead. There is a long silence.)

Justine

Poor man. You have perished by your own principles.

Madame Dubois

He would have perished of starvation much sooner, if he hadn't had those principles. Anyway, by his own words, he enjoyed himself.

Second Man

Hey, I hear a noise.

Third Man

Quick.

(They retreat into the bushes. Two young men enter.)

Young Man

Florent, look. (pointing to the body)

Florent

By all that's holy.

(A shot rings out. The stranger is dead. Florent raises his hands. The bandits come out.)

Florent

I'll give you all my money. Just let me go.

Second Man

Let's see how much you've got.

Third Man

Hey, quite a bit.

Florent

You'll let me go?

Fourth Man

Friend, you know very well that we can't let you live.

Justine

I beg you to spare his life. Do me this one favor, please.

Second Man

You know what we want, sweetheart.

Justine

I shall do anything—yes, anything. This man is my relation. A cousin in fact.

Third Man

Will you satisfy us?

Justine (through her tears)

I will satisfy you all.

Second Man

Let him live. But, he must become one of us. What do you say to that, sir?

Florent

Willingly. Sweet cousin. (hugging Justine; whispering)

Why do you call me cousin?

Justine (aside)

I'll explain that later. I'm a prisoner, too. My name is Justine. Second me in all that I do.

Florent

I shall repay this kindness. I shall marry you.

Justine

All I ask is that you help me find a respectable job.

Florent

Why, I know just the thing.

Madame Dubois

We'd better cut him down.

Second Man

We'll bury him in the morning.

(They cut him down.)

Third Man

No use letting people know we're around.

(The lights begin to dim.)

Second Man

I want you first, Justine.

Justine

Wait till bedtime. (under her breath) Dear God, answer my prayers.

Florent

Are you really going to sleep with them?

Justine

Maybe I can make them quarrel. (to Second Man) I think I shall make you wait till last. There's another I like better.

Second Man

Oh, is that it? Well, you're coming with me first.

Justine

Surely, you'll let me choose? (low) Dear God, I pray to you.

Third Man

Why not let her choose?

Fourth Man

That's right. I can see she likes me the best.

Second Man

I'm boss here.

Justine

God will answer me. (aloud) Why look, I'll throw my scarf, and the one who catches it and brings it to me shall enjoy me. Dear God, forgive these shameless words.

(Justine throws her scarf and the men fall to scuffling.)

Justine (fervently)

God will answer me.

(There is a sound of hoofbeats, and the sky illuminates with a holy light.)

Madame Dubois

Hightail it. I hear hoofbeats.

(The gang runs. Justine and Florent grab guns and fire after them.)

Justine

We'll kill you if you return.

Florent

And, we have your weapons.

Justine

They're gone.

Florent

I doubt they'll come back.

Justine

I've never been so in danger of losing my virtue.

Florent

I'm greatly beholden to you. I wish to repay you. You saved my life.

Justine

And I, to you. You saved my chastity.

Florent

Better give me the gun.

Justine

Oh, here, take it. I am afraid of it anyway.

Florent

Thank you. Now, allow me to express my gratitude to you. Whore! (knocking her down)

Justine

Is this the way you repay my kindness to you?

Florent

Yes. What you did was done only to help yourself in your escape. Why should I feel any gratitude to you? Besides, (smirking) I hate being under obligations to anyone. Come bitch, remove your clothes.

Justine

Sir, you cannot mean to dishonor me.

Florent

Madame, I can, and what's more I do, and what's more, I will.

Justine

Please, in the name of all that's holy—

Florent

We're wasting time. (removing his waistcoat) When you helped me—if it wasn't purely to save your own neck, then it was to satisfy a generous impulse. Now, how in hell can you ask me to be grateful for the pleasure you gave yourself. As if a man as wealthy as I could ever owe anything to a slut like you. As for gratitude—the pride of an elevated soul should never allow itself to be bowed down by an obligation. An obligation humbles the person receiving it. Now that, I take to be a misfortune. Therefore, gratitude is not a virtue, but a vice. It was never nature's intention that one who received a favor should feel gratitude and forgo his rights to the person yielding to the pleasure of obliging him. Do you find such a sentiment among animals?

Justine

Oh, please sir. I cannot argue with you. I am a simple virgin.

Florent

Ah, all the better. I'm really going to sacrifice you now. Besides, I can't stand to have you prattling about your trifling favors. Come now, say your prayers.

Justine

Monster of nature. I give you your life and you take from me what I hold most dear.

Florent

Be more careful next time.

Justine

Holy and majestic being, in this awful moment, you fill my soul with patience to endure. Oh, my protector, I aspire to your goodness and implore your clemency.

(All through her speech Florent has been removing her clothing and caressing her.)

Justine

Behold my woes and sorrows. Oh mighty God, You know that I am innocent. (she stops)

Florent

Don't stop. It's wonderful. The only thing more stimulating that I can imagine would be to take you on the altar during a High Mass with the Pope himself preaching the sermon.

Justine (in anguish)

Dear God, you know I have been betrayed by a man I have done only good to—in accordance with your commandments—

Florent

Ah, we'll need a pillow. Why not that guts over there? (he drags her to the body and forces her to lie on top of it) You sing sweetly, my nightingale. Your sufferings have only begun.

Justine

You will punish him for it.— Oh, my God!

CURTAIN

ACT II

SCENE 4

Five years have passed. The scene is a room in Florent's Château. Justine enters dressed as a maid.

Florent

Where are you, Justine?

Justine

Here, sir.

Florent

Is my mother up?

Justine

No, sir.

Florent

How long have you been with us, child?

Justine

Five years, sir.

Florent

Is it that long since I raped you?

Justine (bitterly)

Yes, sir.

Florent

Come here, don't be so shy.

Justine

Surely, you don't—

Florent

Nonsense. You know I abhor your sex entirely. Do you know, you are the only woman I have ever touched?

Justine (crying)

Oh, no.

Florent

I suppose you're thinking that I'm the only man who has ever touched you. Well, it was an experiment on both our parts—and on mine, frankly it didn't agree. I preferred boys before, and I still do.

Justine

It's a worse sin than what you did to me.

Florent

You know, I suspect you of sentimentalism about me. I think you're in love with me. Are you?

Justine

Yes, sir.

Florent

But, not because you like me; only because I had your virtue. Silly child! All virtue is born on a false premise. What good is virtue if it cannot protect the weak from the tyranny of the strong?

Justine

The strong are not always tyrannous. Think how good your mother is to me.

Florent

Only because I constantly remind her. She boasts about how good she has been to you—but it's my work.

Justine

Oh, sir, don't deprive me of my faith in humanity and my religion.

Florent

Religion! Hogwash. A man announces himself savior—to whom?—the slaves and sluts of a forgotten part of Asia; the fanaticism of this rabble spreads and lo! the most despicable creature, the most awkward lout, the worst charlatan that has ever appeared in history—behold him a leader, behold him, the Son of God! Behold his ravings, his lies consecrated holy dogmas—his inanities, sacred mysteries.

Justine

Oh, sir—

Florent

If there was virtue in the world, couldn't it find a better spokesman than this rascal? Could it not find a means less absurd, a mouth less lewd?

Justine

Think what you say!

Florent

What I say is the result of profound meditation. Close the door.

(Justine closes the door.)

Florent

I want you to swear never to repeat what I am about to say to you.

Justine (hurt)

How can you believe I would betray your confidence?

Florent

Very good. But I want you to realize that it's worth your life if you betray me.

Justine

I shall not.

Florent

Well then, Justine, it's this: I have decided that mama must die.

Justine

Die!

Florent

And you must help me in this enterprise.

Justine

Help you to kill the woman who, after my mother, has done more for me than anyone? No, no! Kill me, if you want to, but don't ask me to do that!

Florent

Justine, knowing your obstinate character, I am not surprised at your refusal. But I fail to see anything wrong in my intentions. One must be philosophic. Man cannot destroy matter. The most he can do is vary its form. And every form is equal in the eyes of nature. What does it matter to nature, that what is today flesh, is tomorrow worms? Can anybody say that the biped is more in nature's eyes than the worm? Since decomposition is necessary to nature's schemes, he who assists her in it, though styled a criminal, is in fact her ally.

Justine

But nature needs life as much as death.

Florent

True. But the passions are means of accomplishing her ends. If she needs life, she plants in us love. But for destruction, lust, ambition, hatred, and murder. Thus you see her economy is maintained by the fluctuations of the passions. Equilibrium can only be preserved through crime or else we should overpopulate the world and die in comradely starvation.

Justine

But, the person you wish to do away with is your own mother.

Florent

Such arguments are frivolous in the eyes of a philosopher. Can such weak ties, the fruit of our gregarious instinct hold water in your eyes?

Justine

The indifference you see in nature is the result of the way you look at it. Is not the heart also part of nature? And does not your heart condemn you?

Florent

Not in the least.

Justine

Remorse will stab you. You will constantly see her image before you—

Florent

Well, I shall be no worse off then, because I constantly see her image now. And that's what I principally object to.

Justine

Oh, sir. Think again. Reconsider.

Florent

I see I am mistaken in you. I shall find someone else. And you will suffer anyway and she must die.

Justine

How can you think I would harm her? For nothing!

Florent

Ah, so that's it. Well, I do not wish you to do her harm for nothing. You shall find me most generous.

Justine

Sir, you are most persuasive.

Florent (kissing her)

You are the only woman I have ever kissed. I knew your charming head could not have remained in darkness forever. Where wisdom could not penetrate, gold could. Strange humanity.

(A servant knocks.)

Florent

Enter.

Servant (entering)

A message for you, sir. (exit, bowing)

Florent

Well, well. My uncle has just died, leaving me a half million francs. Good fortune always comes at once.

Justine

Now, you will not need to kill your mother.

Florent

Don't be ridiculous. I was never in any need to do it. I just want her disposed of. She's cluttered up the earth too long. We'll go ahead as planned. Tomorrow at the latest.

(Florent goes out. A pause. Justine paces up and down, trying to think of a way out. A monk enters.)

Justine

How is my mistress, brother Severino?

Severino (the same actor who plays the Marquis)

Her conscience is in a good state.

Justine

Oh, Father, I beseech you to help us.

Severino

Why child, in what way?

Justine

Master Florent has bribed me to help him murder my mistress.

Severino

Why, this is a most unnatural act for a son of holy church.

Justine

Ay, father, it is. What is to be done? I agreed to help

him only that I might gain time.

Severino

A wise idea, daughter. Dissimulation in a good cause is not evil.

Justine

What must we do?

Severino

You must come with me to the monastery tonight and tell the other brothers. Then, we shall think of something.

Justine

But, couldn't you contact the police?

Severino

The only police are miles away, and besides, they wouldn't act on the allegations of a servant. No, no. You must come to the monastery. Say you are going to confession.

Justine

Very well, father, I shall come.

Severino

Have you told anyone else of this?

Justine

No one.

Severino

Be sure you don't. That would spoil everything. Now, I must make haste, child.

BLACKOUT

ACT II

SCENE 5

A large cell in the monastery, later that evening. Justine is seated before four darkly robed monks.

Severino

It is a strange story you tell.

Justine

It is true. I swear it on my faith.

Second Monk

I am loath to believe it of young Florent.

Third Monk

He is too well bred.

Justine

I swear it is true.

Fourth Monk

Who would believe her?

Second Monk

Girl, Florent is one of the oldest names in this country.

Third Monk

The most respected.

Fourth Monk

The most devout in its payments to holy church.

Severino

Nay, but brothers, I believe her.

Second Monk

And I.

Third Monk

And I.

Fourth Monk

And I.

Justine

Then, you will help?

Severino

I never said that.

Second Monk

Nor I.

Third Monk

Nor I.

Fourth Monk

Nor I.

Justine

But, why then did you bring me here and listen to me?

Severino

Shall I tell her?

All

Ay, tell her.

Severino

Open the door.

(The Fourth Monk opens the door. In stalks Florent.)

Florent

So, you've betrayed me, you bitch!! Well, it has done you no good. My mother has been dead for an hour and the alarm is out for you. It's thought you poisoned her.

Justine

Ah, poor lady—

Florent

But, no one knows you are here. And, no one ever will. You see, I know of the practices of these good friars. Everyone will believe you guilty, and so you cannot escape. Whilst my friends, the monks, initiate you into the mysteries of their most secret religion.

Severino

Explain the mysteries to her.

Second Monk

We are a sect of the religion of Sham, novice: listen well.

Third Monk

We practice the sternest discipline.

Fourth Monk

We mortify the flesh.

(They all pull out whips from beneath their tunics.)

Severino

Not our own, of course.

Second Monk

Scourge her.

(They whip her savagely while delivering the following sermon.)

Second Monk

We live here in holy retirement.

Third Monk

Each of us has a female servant.

Fourth Monk

Who ministers to all our needs.

Severino

And we have taken a vow against poverty—thus we have many needs.

Second Monk

And the girl remains with us until we tire of her.

Third Monk

And then, if no one else chooses her, she is reformed.

Fourth Monk

Reformed.

Severino

Reformed.

Florent

Which, to speak plainly, means she has her throat cut at a Black Mass held especially for the purpose. This is pleasant, gentlemen, but I must arrange Mama's funeral. I leave you, Justine, to the punishment you deserve for betraying me. Ah, I would have made you rich if you had not fallen into the temptation of virtue. Adieu, holy fathers.

(Florent exits.)

Severino

Salve, sir.

Second Monk

Bless you, my son.

Third Monk

Blessings be on your house.

Fourth Monk

Go, true son of the Church.

Justine

Oh, sweet gentlemen, in the name of religion—

Second Monk

Surely, you don't expect to find that here?

Third Monk

Don't you know that the closer you get to the church, the farther you get from religion?

Severino

There is nothing you could say that could rouse our violence more.

Justine

Jesus Christ, protect me—

Severino

Blasphemer!

Second Monk

Let me kill her.

Third Monk

Oh, the most untimely words ever spoken.

Fourth Monk

Provoking woman. You trifle too long with human patience. Do you think we are saints?

Severino (whipping her)

In the name of the Father—

Second Monk (whipping her)

In the name of the Son—

Third Monk (whipping her)

In the name of the Holy Ghost—

All

Whip her!

Justine

How can you so desecrate the cloth?

Severino

Why, child, you must realize, lamb, that the interests of the clergy and the interests of religion are diametrically opposed.

Second Monk

And always have been and always will be.

Third Monk

The clergy have always crucified the religious, the saintly, the pious.

Severino

And will.

Fourth Monk

And must!

Second Monk

For, how else is the sanctity of religion to be tested?

Third Monk

By trials, lamb, by trials.

Fourth Monk

And we shall provide you many trials.

Severino

Ah, she is a sweet wench.

Second Monk

How the lamb will bleed.

Justine

Cruel men, how can you enjoy torturing me like this?

Third Monk

The most ridiculous thing in the world is to dispute differences of taste.

Severino

Differences in taste spring from differences in natural constitutions.

Fourth Monk

Hence, are not acquired.

Severino

Hence, are completely relative.

Second Monk

Hence, cannot be changed but by perverting nature.

Third Monk

It is like asking a tall man to be short.

Severino

She is not altogether stupid. I shall reason with her, put her through the catechism, as it were. Answer, lamb, as I question you. (in a sing song voice) You think our tastes are unnatural?

Justine (flat)

They are, at least, unusual.

Severino (sing-song)

Only to your way of think-ing.

Justine (flat)

I think as most men think.

Severino (sing-song)

You think you think as most men think. But you are mis-taken!

Justine

That cannot be, sir!

Severino

Some men like soup. Some men like tea. But a torturer, I would be.

Justine (singing)

A good man would not.

Severino

A good man or villain is born such. It would be a sacrilege to try to improve nature.

Second Monk

When anatomy is truly perfected, it will be shown that morality is essentially a matter of physics.

Justine

But, if this is so, why do kings punish you for your crimes?

Third Monk

It is unjust, to be sure, but is an added perversity of the human group that it cannot tolerate invention.

Fourth Monk

And when invention is applied to pleasure, this is most hated.

Severino

Behold us, martyrs of an unjust persecution.

Justine

How can you bear making others unhappy to gain your pleasures?

Second Monk

It is the orgasm that is important. And that can be improved considerably without sharing it with the woman. In fact, it may be possible to improve it only at the expense of the woman.

Severino

There is a lot of sentimental nonsense today that a man should not be happy unless the woman shares his paroxysm. As if the instrument of pleasure were important. Thus, we should not eat lest the spoon enjoy, the cook, the waiter. What drivel!

Third Monk

It is only a false pride that begets such nonsense. It goes hand in hand with romance, but it has nothing to do with the pleasures of true love.

Justine

With ideas like these you will turn out to be murderers.

Severino

So be it. I shall be faithful to nature's commands. In so doing, I shall serve God. The wolf who devours the lamb serves God as well as the lamb who is devoured.

Justine

I refuse to admit it.

Second Monk

That's because you don't want to be the lamb.

Severino

Unheard of selfishness.

Third Monk

If you were the wolf, you'd understand. Ask the wolf what is the purpose of the lamb. He will say, 'To feed me,' just as humans say that all animals are here for that purpose. It would be more correct to say we are here to feed each other.

Justine

If there were no crimes against nature, whence comes this repugnance we feel?

Severino

From want of habit. It is like food. We dislike it because we have not acquired a taste for it.

Third Monk

The greater the crime, the greater the utility of it to nature's scheme.

Justine

Horrid, horrible men.

Severino

She is hopeless.

Second Monk

Say rather, she is lost.

Third Monk

She is in a state of sin.

Severino

Let us dress her as the Virgin Mary and lead her to the altar, there to imitate by turns, God the Father, cuckolding his faithful servant, Joseph.

Second Monk

I feel I have in me the makings of a new redeemer.

Third Monk

Come wench, you are about to be made blessed among women.

(They drive her out with whips as the curtain falls.)

CURTAIN

ACT III

SCENE 6

Doctor Rodin's laboratory. The place resembles an alchemist's nightmare, with test tubes running all about, and a human skeleton to one side.

Justine

Oh, Rosalie, how can you say your father is cruel?

Rosalie

I say it because it is true.

Justine

But, how can he be cruel? Doctor Rodin saved me from those loathsome monks.

Rosalie

Only because he has a nausea of anything religious—a nausea that extends even to black magic.

Justine

But, if he is cruel, why does he keep a charitable school for orphans?

Rosalie

So that he may whip the students when they misbehave in class or fail in their lessons. You don't know how he whipped me before he hit upon the idea of that school.

Justine

Rosalie, I refuse to listen. I refuse to believe your father is like all the rest. Hasn't he devoted his life to scientific research to save human life?

Rosalie (ironically)

Oh, he has performed no end of—experiments.

Rodin (entering)

Run along, Rosalie, I want to talk to Justine.

Rosalie

Beware. (Rosalie obediently runs off)

Rodin

How are your wounds, Justine, all healed?

Justine

Yes, thanks to you. But for you, those wicked priests would have marked me for life.

Rodin

Ah, to what excesses will not religious fanaticism lead misguided men?

Justine

They were demonists, not truly religious men—they only hid their cruelties behind the face of religion. They were pretenders.

Rodin

Demoniacs—saints—what is the difference? Only that the saint belongs to the established church. The label signifies approval. But the goods are the same.

Justine

Ah, sir, I wish your kindness extended to religion.

Rodin

Let us pass over such nonsense. I should prefer to be kind to you.

Justine

You have been kind—

Rodin

But, I wish to express my feelings in a more biological way.

Justine

I have but little money, but take it, let me leave your house.

Rodin

But, I am not asking you to be my mistress—

Justine

Then, I mistook you. Oh, how sorry I am. Forgive me.

Rodin

Of course, child. What I want you to do is to become my assistant.

Justine

Willingly, sir.

Rodin

Do not agree too rapidly, Justine. Remember, today science is persecuted by prejudice. Our experiments, to some, may seem sacrilegious.

Justine

I am sure you would do nothing wrong.

Rodin (emphatically)

Nothing wrong can be done in the interests of science, child. That's the point. Experimentation is good per se. By experiment we copy nature, we learn her ways. What can be nobler than imitating nature? Consider the tarantula, the black widow spider as examples of the nobility of nature.

Justine (not really comprehending)

Yes, sir.

Rodin

I know there are those who would inhibit experimentation because of the results to which it leads. There are some who condemn the scientists, who laboring long and hard, discovered arsenic—a drug that has both beneficial and evil properties. As if it were the scientists' fault that nature's sword is double edged. No, they would rather remain in ignorance and superstition. Pathetic creatures!

Justine

But, why do you honor me with such confidence?

Rodin

I shall be very frank, charming girl. The experiment I propose to undertake might be frowned upon by the reactionary and priest-ridden authorities of our misgoverned country. Now, a scientific mind cannot be governed by their lunacies. However, a scientific mind may take precautions. I choose you because I believe you will be both intelligent and silent.

Justine

I shall try to be both, sir.

Rodin

Good girl. I knew you could do it. Now, I have two projects most dear to my heart. The first is to breed a new species of animal by crossing several diverse species.

Justine

But, that has been done before.

Rodin

Not with the species I propose to employ. It is a common prejudice that human beings cannot bear the offspring of animals. This silly prejudice prevails despite historical reports from all over the world to the contrary. A prejudice that would long ago have vanished but for the sinister preoccupations of the clergy in their efforts to treat man as a unique form of nature.

Justine (aside)

Abominable! What do I hear?

Rodin

I propose to settle the matter once and for all.

Justine

H-how, sir?

Rodin

By experimentation, of course! Nothing else will satisfy the demands of a scientific age.

Justine

Oh—

Rodin

I propose to make the attempt with a monkey. Think of the benefit to mankind that will result. We shall have for the first time a truly sub-human species of domestic animal that nonetheless can understand and perform all our commands, without however, of having the disagreeable trait of demanding equality and integration.

Justine

And on whom do you propose to try this—experiment?

Rodin

Why, on you, Justine, on you.

Justine

I should have guessed. Somehow, I should have guessed.

Rodin

I, myself, shall perform the reverse experiment with a female monkey.

Justine

It sounds more like the past every minute. I could have

predicted it, surely.

Rodin

I have another project that is dearer to my heart at the moment. What I have just told you is for the future.

Justine

I just can't wait to hear it.

Rodin

Anatomy, child, is the queen of the sciences. Alas, it has not yet been perfected. Mainly this is because dissection has been confined to corpses. Never will it attain the last degree of perfection until an examination is made of a living subject.

Justine (ironically)

Oh, well. Why not use your daughter?

Rodin

Exactly my intention! She is a disappointment to me intellectually, but she has lovely veins.

Justine

I thought you might hesitate about your own daughter. I see I misjudged you.

Rodin

Should silly considerations of family hinder the progress of science? I dedicated my life to humanity. Have great men ever allowed themselves to be subject to such degrading ties? When Michelangelo wanted to paint Christ crucified, did he hesitate to crucify a man and copy his agonies? How much more important is our case: We sacrifice one person to save millions. Hesitation would be criminal.

Justine

'Our case?'

Rodin

Yes, we, child—you and I, for I count you as one of us. One dedicated to the advancement of science. We shall march shoulder to shoulder. In the many hospitals I have worked in there have been many such experiments, but, alas, not conducted under properly controlled conditions. This is what I hope to improve. Our names shall be famous, Justine. And do not think I shall hesitate to share the glory with you. No, child, we shall share it equally.

Justine

I confess I am still amazed that you find it so easy to throw off the ties of affection—

Rodin

Why, because she is my daughter? I gave her life, I may take it away. It is a right recognized by all nations until this execrable Jewish superstition overwhelmed the world. And even today, does not the well- being of the nation depend on the servitude of the children? Who else do we send to war? The old are physically unfit, and far too wise. And, in our case, think of the benefit to humanity. It is this goal I see. Since I sacrifice myself to it, why may I not sacrifice my daughter? As for the ties of parental love, (scoffing) they are beneath the notice of a philosopher.

Rosalie (enters)

Father, there is someone to see you.

Justine

Fly, Rosalie, fly. Your father means to vivisect you.

Rosalie

I knew it all along. (she runs off)

Rodin

Monster! Hypocrite! Betrayer of trust! Superstitious witch! It is not enough that you retard science, but you rob a father of his daughter? (striking Justine) Slut! I should ravish you, but I have too little time. I shall content myself with branding you. I have a new method. (pulling an iron from his desk) Instead of fire, I use acid. It lasts longer, of course. Here, wench. (he brands her and she screams) Ah, it really works. Now, I shall mate you with a gorilla.

(Justine faints.)

Blackout

ACT III
SCENE 7

A surreal prison. To the right a gallows; in the center, bars representing Justine's cell, to the left a man broken on a wheel. Justine is in her cell praying. The stage illuminates and Madame Dubois enters, rigged out as a countess.

Justine

Why, your excellency, why have you come to this humble cell?

Countess

I have heard of your sad plight, child. And I, Countess Walewska, thought I might be able to help you.

Justine

No one believes I am innocent because I have been branded. No one will listen. I have prayed God—

Countess

I believe you, Justine, and I will use my influence to have you released.

Justine

You are so good. So unlike the rest—

Countess

On one condition—

Justine (aside)

Here it comes.

Countess

But first—don't you recognize me?

Justine

Can it be? Madame Dubois.

Countess

Countess Walewska now.

Justine

But how you must have reformed!

Madame Dubois

Reformed! Don't be a fool. If I'd been good—I'd have wound up like you—or worse. You see these diamonds—this silk—this title—what do you think they cost me?

Justine

Oh, a great deal.

Madame Dubois

Not a bit. Stole 'em! All of 'em! But, I'm a real countess nonetheless. The title was obtained fraudulently, but that doesn't matter. I've had it too long to lose it.

Justine

You'll never change.

Madame Dubois

And why should I? So I can exchange my title for your brand?

Justine (crying)

Do not mock me.

Madame Dubois

I'm sorry, child. I don't like to be mean. But somehow, I must persuade you out of this inconvenient virtue of yours. It's not a question of following the good and shunning evil—it's simply a matter of following the fashion. And vice is the fashion these days—and has been as long as I can remember.

Justine

Oh, but—

Madame Dubois

Child, never fight public opinion.

Justine

But, if everyone believed as you do—what then?

Madame Dubois

Well, as a matter of fact, I think everyone does, though they take care not to admit it.

Justine

What you advocate would be a war of all against all. Think of the danger you would run.

Madame Dubois

But I would be consoled by the knowledge that I make everyone else run the same risk. Thus, I would establish a perfect equality among men—an equality of the only type they are likely to enjoy.

Justine

But, think of remorse.

Madame Dubois

Why bother? Remorse can be quenched very easily. It stems from want of habit. If you suffer from remorse from anything you do—the remedy is simple: do it again and again. You'll be amazed how quickly your conscience is relieved. Repetition is better than confession.

Justine (coldly)

Tell me your condition.

Madame Dubois

Justine, I have always wished you well, despite the trick you played me a few years ago—and I thought, well, I thought—I thought, perhaps you might be tired of being raped and mistreated by men—the beasts—and that you might prefer—since you must assuredly be someone's victim with your character—to try the ministrations of a woman. In a word—mine. I have always liked you, Justine—and I will be very kind—

Justine

Get out. I'd rather die first.

Madame Dubois

Very well! I'll see to it that you shall. The judge is a friend of mine— (she exits)

(Justine prays; the stage illumines, and in walks one of the monks.)

Justine

Brother Martin!

Monk

No, it's I, brother Luther.

Justine

Why are you here?

Monk

I am come to confess you, child.

Justine

In that case, I'd rather die unshriven.

Monk

Ah, child, it's a hard case, and there's no reprieve—that's sure. But, don't harden your heart against the church. That's a sin.

Justine

In my eyes, you do not represent the church.

Monk

I am an ordained priest. Do you question the Pope's authority? Are you a heretic as well?

Justine

You disgrace the cloth.

Monk

But, I wear it with every bit as much right as a saint. And, would you inquire into the rights of authority?

Justine (defiantly)

Yes!

Monk

A self-confessed heretic. If I tell them, they will burn you.

Justine

Tell them, do. It would be just like you.

Monk

Why lamb, I want to save you.

Justine (dumbfounded)

Save me?

Monk

Ay, lamb.

Justine (cagily)

On what condition?

Monk

Why, no condition, Justine.

Justine

That's a surprise.

Monk

I will simply take you under the authority of holy church, and you will have sanctuary at my monastery.

Justine

I knew it. I'll never go back there.

Monk

But, it's a new monastery, lamb, not the old moth-eaten one you were at before, but a new one designed by me.

Justine

By you?

Monk

Yes, lamb, they wouldn't make me Pope as it were, so I decided I'd play in my own arena.

Justine

If you play the same kind of games, I'll never go.

(Luther begins to strip her clothes off.)

Monk

I've invented a new game, (caressing her) several new

games— Isn't this better than death?

Justine

No.

Monk

Very well, lamb. I'll see to it they burn you. Better say nothing of this, or I'll swear you enticed me.

(Brother Luther exits. Justine prays. Luther meets the Judge (the same actor who played Florent) and whispers to him. As if in answer to her prayer, the stage illumines again and the Judge enters, accompanied by a masked hangman.)

Justine

Oh, your honor, I am not guilty.

Florent

And, if you are not guilty, who is? You are accused of poisoning my mother, of theft, of being a whore, and last, but not least, of being a heretic. You have consorted with thieves, murderers and heretics all your life. Now, why aren't you guilty, eh?

Justine

You, yourself, know I am innocent of one of the

charges.

Florent

True, but that does not mean you should not be punished.

Justine

Is that what must happen to a girl whose only offense is her poverty and helplessness?

Florent

Therein lies your crime.

Justine

How can that be?

Florent

Because nature does not intend that poverty be alleviated. If it were, it would be more tolerable and that would increase the likelihood that it will continue. No, poverty is a capital crime. Nature has chosen that one must either rise above it or perish. And no worse aberration exists than that known as socialism and charity which disturbs nature's sublime arrangements in the name of humanity. Nature intended the weak to be ruled by the strong. But civilization replaced strength with wealth. Observe, however, that a priority of power remains unaffected. Nature does not care who is crushed so long as some be crushed. It is our moral duty as individuals to avoid that. To fail is to be guilty. You, Justine, have been deplorably deficient in that regard— Therefore, you are guilty—

Hangman

Guilty, my lord.

Justine

What, of virtue, benevolence, humanity?

Florent

Stumbling blocks on the road to happiness.

Justine

How unhappy would be mankind if society were as cruel as you pretend.

Florent

Think how unhappy it is. In society as it is now foolishly constituted, natural acts are prohibited as crimes. Thus, not only are the victims of crime unhappy, but contrary to nature's plan, so are the perpetrators who are made to pay dearly for their pleasures. Now, if crime were to be permitted as nature intended, only the victims would be unhappy and those without criminal inclinations would be indifferent. The only truly happy society is a criminal society.

Justine

Wicked, cynical man.

Florent

I came not in cynicism, but to help you.

Justine

I don't believe it.

Florent

I am prepared to dismiss your case.

Justine

Provided, what?

Florent

Justine, you see I am a wealthy and respected man. I nonetheless possess the same inclinations as when you knew me. I require two boys a day now. My wealth permits me a certain leeway, but I must employ agents. Because of my power to create poverty in this city—for it is poverty that drives young children into the streets, I can usually supply my needs. Once I had to create a famine to keep the supply fresh, but though it took a little manipulating, it repaid the effort many times over. Not merely in pleasure for me, but in profits. It drove some upper class boys into the streets and the resale value—

Justine

Monster!

Florent

What I need is a woman with a keen eye—one who knows poverty herself—who can spot fresh talent like a market woman after green sprouts.

Justine

Never, never, never! May I die first.

Florent

Same old Justine. These, Justine, are the instruments of Justice. (a man is hanged on the gibbet, another is pulled apart on the rack) Is it not amazing the cunning man incorporates into such instruments? They contain more human ingenuity than a Gothic Cathedral. And, far more useful. They express man's nature. Yes, if murder is the delicacy of nature, then judicial murder is the refinement of civilization. Consider that it is on murder alone that civilization finally rests. It occurs to me that society is just one masterful crime. And the most daring of all because it proclaims its crimes as

Justice. How many men does civilization kill and sanctify the deed? How many that are no more than social misfits, altogether harmless? How many boys perish in its useless laws? How many die for its numberless causes?

Justine

Think on your own crimes.

Florent

I do. And I see how pure and innocent I am; for I have never committed a crime but to satisfy a need, a pleasure. Can civilization say as much?

Justine

Will you kill me?

Florent

Hangman, tell her what you like to do.

Hangman

I like—I like— Neck,—neck—chop—and, and— (he is feebleminded)

Florent

He means to say—he is a moron and cannot express

himself well—he means to say that he likes to decapitate a woman and deflower the corpse.

Justine

Good God!

Florent

He's not highly sublimated, but he's an efficient creature, the best hangman we've ever had, so we put up with his eccentricities. It is up to you, whether you prefer that he desecrates your body before, during or after the execution. He's sure of his reward in any case. And it may be said that he cares little when he takes it. A live woman excites him no more—and no less—than a headless one. They all excite him—.

Hangman

I want—I like—give you—BABOOM-BABOOM!

Justine

Don't let him touch me until I am dead.

Florent

As you wish, dear. Anything to please you.

Justine

Let me pray. (falling to her knees) Dear God, I pray to you once again. Have I not resisted all temptations and remained pure? Have I not behaved like Job? If there is consolation to be offered a poor creature like me, I pray for it.

Florent

That will do. Hangman, do your duty.

Hangman (raising his ax)

Pretty neck. Soon all blood. I lick while I BABOOM-BABOOM.

(Suddenly the stage illumines and M. de Corville and Juliette enter. Heavenly music seems to play. Shouts are heard: "A rescue! A rescue!")

M. de Corville

Stop, in the name of the King!

Hangman

You mean I can't—?

M. de Corville

You shall have work presently, sir. Be patient.

Florent

And, who are you?

M. de Corville

I am Hyppolyte-Auguste Nemours de Corville, Comte de Villefranche, Vicomte de Fleury, Master of the Rolls, Lieutenant General to the King—and lover to Mademoiselle Juliette, whom I have the honor to let beat me, and whose foot I kiss—religieusement.

Florent

Your servant, sir.

Juliette

My baby sister, what have they done to you?

Justine

I am happy in my reunion with you, dearest.

Florent

For all that, how dare you interfere with justice?

M. de Corville

I have a pardon from the King for Mademoiselle Justine, which I procured with my own hand.

Juliette

Poor Justine. I have heard of all your misfortunes and sufferings. I will have your enemies punished, never fear.

Florent (reading the pardon, gasping)

Surely, this is a joke?

M. de Corville

Well, it is a trifle amusing, I admit.

Florent (staggered)

On what grounds?

M. de Corville

The murder of your mother, of course.

Florent

But, a trial?

M. de Corville

A tedious formality that we thought a philosopher, such as yourself, would dispense with. We mean to hang you, sir, and you know the King in France need not bother with a trial.

Hangman (gleefully)

You mean I can—?

M. de Corville

Right now if you please.

Hangman (gesturing)

And can I—?

Florent (bravely)

Well, what difference does it make how you perish to any rational creature. A gibbet—on the battlefield— All's one.

Justine

Spare him.

Juliette

Never!

M. de Corville

Justice must take its course, child.

(Florent is dispatched on the gibbet by a rather frisky and perhaps randy hangman.)

Justine (covering her face)

Oh, Juliette, how thankful I am to be reunited with you.

Juliette

Poor darling. This should teach you the pernicious effects of your fanatic morality.

Justine

But, it is through God's Grace that I am rescued.

Juliette

God's Grace! Ridiculous! It is through my having slept with every influential man in Paris—including the King—and through the devotion of my slave here.

M. de Corville

My Queen.

Juliette

It is because your sister is a whore that she has been able to obtain your pardon.

Justine

Oh, horrible. I should rather die than be rescued by my

sister's shame.

(The stage suddenly blackens. There is a tremendous crash of thunder and a flash of lightning.)

A Voice (resonant enough to be the voice of God)

Will you never learn, unhappy girl? My patience is at an end.

(The lights go up slowly. Justine is dead.)

M. de Corville

Struck by lightning. Right in the heart.

Juliette (weeping)

My baby sister. It was false doctrine that did this to her. Help me with her, slave.

M. de Corville

Wait, my Queen. You know I am in the habit of reflecting deeply on nature. Leave her there. I want to inscribe a sharp impression on my mind. I deduce from this the unhappy effects of defying God's will.

CURTAIN

EPILOGUE
SCENE 8

M. de Sade reappears.

De Sade

There, ladies and gentlemen, there! How can anyone accuse me of immorality and insanity now? Surely Justine is resplendent in her defiant virtue. (pause)

The design of this drama is undoubtedly unique. Vice is shown everywhere triumphant and virtue the victim of its own sacrifices— But the purpose, ladies and gentlemen, was to ennoble—to inspire faith. Can I not hear you saying "Oh, how these crimes make me love virtue—how sublime she is in her tears." It is in order to guard against such dangerous sophisms, such as vice is punished and virtue is rewarded, that I have written this entertainment. It is in order to make you love virtue that I have presented it to you bleeding, as it were, sure that in this aspect it would appear more pleasing in your eyes. And the fact that Heaven struck down Justine must be attributed to the mysterious ways of God, rather than to the false conclusions drawn by

M. de Corville.

In no way would I want you to identify with the words and actions of the heinous characters in this play. Thank you very much. I hope you have enjoyed this morality. Please tell the warden and the doctors I am sane—if you liked the play, of course—

Ladies and Gentlemen, (bowing) good night.

ABOUT THE AUTHOR

Frank J. Morlock has written and translated many plays since retiring from the legal profession in 1992. His translations have also appeared on Project Gutenberg, the Alexandre Dumas Père web page, Literature in the Age of Napoléon, Infinite Artistries.com, and Munsey's (formerly Blackmask). In 2006 he received an award from the North American Jules Verne Society for his translations of Verne's plays. He lives and works in México.

www.ingramcontent.com/pod-product-compliance
Lightning Source LLC
La Vergne TN
LVHW091308080426
835510LV00007B/422